Hello Awesome:

You are fucking amazing.

And this planner will help you enjoy
the kickass year that you deserve.

The *Fresh Out of Fucks Planner* is filled with funny
motivational quotes, calendars and checklists
that will brighten the fuck out of your day and
help you crush your goals.

Are you ready to say?

 Fuck YES! to... **Fuck NO! to...**

Fuck YES! to...	Fuck NO! to...
Loving the fuck out of yourself	Being a bitch to yourself
Saving your fucks for important shit	Assholes and bullshit
Getting shit done	Shitshows and overwhelm
Laughing your ass off	Boring affirmations

Okay then, you beautiful, uncensored,
unstoppable badass!

let's fucking go!

Fresh Out of Fucks 2025: Sweary Planner With Funny Affirmations & Motivational Quotes

Sassy Quotes Press
Helping badass women laugh and get shit done since 2021

ISBN: 978-1-957633-51-0

Questions? Comments?

I would love to hear from you! Please email Jen@SassyQuotesPress.com

Ready for your fabulous Bonus Gifts?

Go to the **Bonus Gifts** page at the back of this book for instant access download info.

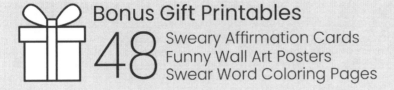

Bonus Gift Printables

48 Sweary Affirmation Cards
Funny Wall Art Posters
Swear Word Coloring Pages

Sign up for more freebies and updates at SASSYQUOTESPRESS.COM

This Belongs to:

_____

_____

_____

_____

_____

_____

2025

JANUARY

S	M	T	W	T	F	S
			1	2	3	4
5	6	7	8	9	10	11
12	13	14	15	16	17	18
19	20	21	22	23	24	25
26	27	28	29	30	31	

FEBRUARY

S	M	T	W	T	F	S
						1
2	3	4	5	6	7	8
9	10	11	12	13	14	15
16	17	18	19	20	21	22
23	24	25	26	27	28	

MARCH

S	M	T	W	T	F	S
						1
2	3	4	5	6	7	8
9	10	11	12	13	14	15
16	17	18	19	20	21	22
23	24	25	26	27	28	29
30	31					

APRIL

S	M	T	W	T	F	S
		1	2	3	4	5
6	7	8	9	10	11	12
13	14	15	16	17	18	19
20	21	22	23	24	25	26
27	28	29	30			

MAY

S	M	T	W	T	F	S
				1	2	3
4	5	6	7	8	9	10
11	12	13	14	15	16	17
18	19	20	21	22	23	24
25	26	27	28	29	30	31

JUNE

S	M	T	W	T	F	S
1	2	3	4	5	6	7
8	9	10	11	12	13	14
15	16	17	18	19	20	21
22	23	24	25	26	27	28
29	30					

JULY

S	M	T	W	T	F	S
		1	2	3	4	5
6	7	8	9	10	11	12
13	14	15	16	17	18	19
20	21	22	23	24	25	26
27	28	29	30	31		

AUGUST

S	M	T	W	T	F	S
					1	2
3	4	5	6	7	8	9
10	11	12	13	14	15	16
17	18	19	20	21	22	23
24	25	26	27	28	29	30
31						

SEPTEMBER

S	M	T	W	T	F	S
	1	2	3	4	5	6
7	8	9	10	11	12	13
14	15	16	17	18	19	20
21	22	23	24	25	26	27
28	29	30				

OCTOBER

S	M	T	W	T	F	S
			1	2	3	4
5	6	7	8	9	10	11
12	13	14	15	16	17	18
19	20	21	22	23	24	25
26	27	28	29	30	31	

NOVEMBER

S	M	T	W	T	F	S
						1
2	3	4	5	6	7	8
9	10	11	12	13	14	15
16	17	18	19	20	21	22
23	24	25	26	27	28	29
30						

DECEMBER

S	M	T	W	T	F	S
	1	2	3	4	5	6
7	8	9	10	11	12	13
14	15	16	17	18	19	20
21	22	23	24	25	26	27
28	29	30	31			

2026

JANUARY

S	M	T	W	T	F	S
				1	2	3
4	5	6	7	8	9	10
11	12	13	14	15	16	17
18	19	20	21	22	23	24
25	26	27	28	29	30	31

FEBRUARY

S	M	T	W	T	F	S
1	2	3	4	5	6	7
8	9	10	11	12	13	14
15	16	17	18	19	20	21
22	23	24	25	26	27	28

MARCH

S	M	T	W	T	F	S
1	2	3	4	5	6	7
8	9	10	11	12	13	14
15	16	17	18	19	20	21
22	23	24	25	26	27	28
29	30	31				

APRIL

S	M	T	W	T	F	S
			1	2	3	4
5	6	7	8	9	10	11
12	13	14	15	16	17	18
19	20	21	22	23	24	25
26	27	28	29	30		

MAY

S	M	T	W	T	F	S
					1	2
3	4	5	6	7	8	9
10	11	12	13	14	15	16
17	18	19	20	21	22	23
24	25	26	27	28	29	30
31						

JUNE

S	M	T	W	T	F	S
	1	2	3	4	5	6
7	8	9	10	11	12	13
14	15	16	17	18	19	20
21	22	23	24	25	26	27
28	29	30				

JULY

S	M	T	W	T	F	S
			1	2	3	4
5	6	7	8	9	10	11
12	13	14	15	16	17	18
19	20	21	22	23	24	25
26	27	28	29	30	31	

AUGUST

S	M	T	W	T	F	S
						1
2	3	4	5	6	7	8
9	10	11	12	13	14	15
16	17	18	19	20	21	22
23	24	25	26	27	28	29
30	31					

SEPTEMBER

S	M	T	W	T	F	S
		1	2	3	4	5
6	7	8	9	10	11	12
13	14	15	16	17	18	19
20	21	22	23	24	25	26
27	28	29	30			

OCTOBER

S	M	T	W	T	F	S
				1	2	3
4	5	6	7	8	9	10
11	12	13	14	15	16	17
18	19	20	21	22	23	24
25	26	27	28	29	30	31

NOVEMBER

S	M	T	W	T	F	S
1	2	3	4	5	6	7
8	9	10	11	12	13	14
15	16	17	18	19	20	21
22	23	24	25	26	27	28
29	30					

DECEMBER

S	M	T	W	T	F	S
		1	2	3	4	5
6	7	8	9	10	11	12
13	14	15	16	17	18	19
20	21	22	23	24	25	26
27	28	29	30	31		

✔ Fuck YES! Goals & Shit

What goals do you want to crush with your awesomeness? Self care, relationships, hobbies, work? Your possibilities are endless.

_____

_____

_____

_____

_____

_____

_____

_____

_____

_____

_____

_____

_____

_____

_____

_____

_____

_____

_____

☒ Fuck NO! Bullshit

The best way to let more happiness into your life is to get rid of soul-sucking fuckery. Toxic people, negative thoughts, perfectionism and other shit can fuck off! What bullshit will you trash?

_____

_____

_____

_____

_____

_____

_____

_____

_____

_____

_____

_____

_____

_____

_____

_____

_____

☒ Fuck NO! Assholes

You can do hard things, but putting up with assholes shouldn't be one of them! With this handy list of insults and comebacks, you'll always have a creative way to say "Fuck off!"

1. You're about as useful as shit-scented deodorant.

2. I wouldn't say that you're a huge asshole, but YOUR anus is also bigger than Pluto.

3. I don't wish you were dead. I just think your breathing is excessive.

4. You're not "butt ugly," but your face does make penises look good.

5. You're so full of shit, your doorbell says "ding dung."

6. That's cute. You think you're the personality hire, but we know you're the dumpster fire.

7. Check your phone. I think you forgot to take it off Asshole Mode.

8. I wouldn't say you're an idiot, but your brain does identify as a rock.

9. To the world, you are an asshole. But to me, you are also an asshole.

10. "WTF!?," you ask? Your guess is as good as mine, but your ass is not.

11. Annoying the shit out of people is NOT a love language.

12. I'm trying to understand what you're saying, but Google translate is just giving me fart sounds.

13. You are what you eat, and you're clearly a poop-ivore.

14. Being a huge asshole and people liking you is not a thing.

15. I'm not gaslighting you. I think you're just breathing your own farts.

16. You're so dumb, you shouldn't even be allowed to own finger guns.

17. I hate to disappoint you, but... oh wait, it's actually quite nice.

18. I'm done practicing gratitude. I'm so fucking grateful that I'm not you, I've gone pro.

19. You're the whole package: a total dick.

20. Let's play a fun game of "Hide-and-Go-Fuck-Yourself."

21. They say that absence makes the heart grow fonder, so we'd love it if you'd go the fuck away.

22. I wouldn't say you're a dumbass. But wisdom-free is fair.

23. At least there's a method to your madness. Fuck up, rinse, repeat.

24. It doesn't take a rocket scientist to wish you were living on Mars.

25. With all due respect, fuck you.

2025 Plan

- ☑ **LIVE** your badass life
- ☑ **LAUGH** your ass off
- ☑ **LOVE** the fuck out of yourself

let's fucking go!

December-January 2025

30 Monday

31 Tuesday
New Year's Eve

1 Wednesday
New Year's Day

Important as fuck

Fucking grateful for…

New year, same Fuck It era!

2 Thursday

_____
_____
_____
_____
_____
_____
_____
_____
_____
_____
_____
_____
_____

○ _____
○ _____
○ _____
○ _____
○ _____
○ _____
○ _____
○ _____
○ _____

3 Friday

_____
_____
_____
_____
_____
_____
_____
_____
_____
_____
_____

○ _____
○ _____
○ _____
○ _____
○ _____
○ _____
○ _____
○ _____
○ _____

4 Saturday

_____
_____
_____
_____
_____
_____
○ _____
○ _____
○ _____

5 Sunday

_____
_____
_____
_____
_____
○ _____
○ _____
○ _____

Notes and shit

_____
_____
_____

January 2025

Sunday	Monday	Tuesday	Wednesday
DECEMBER 2024 S M T W T F S 1 2 3 4 5 6 7 8 9 10 11 12 13 14 15 16 17 18 19 20 21 22 23 24 25 26 27 28 29 30 31	**FEBRUARY 2025** S M T W T F S 1 2 3 4 5 6 7 8 9 10 11 12 13 14 15 16 17 18 19 20 21 22 23 24 25 26 27 28		1 New Year's Day
5	6	7	8
12	13	14	15
19	20 Martin Luther King Jr. Day (US), Inauguration Day (US)	21	22
26	27 Australia Day (AU)	28	29 Chinese New Year

You pay your fucking dues. So own your fucking awesomeness.

Thursday	Friday	Saturday	Important shit
2	3	4	_____
			_____
			_____
			_____
9	10	11	_____
			_____
			_____
			_____
16	17	18	_____
			_____
			_____
			_____
23	24	25	_____
			_____
			_____
			_____
30	31		_____
			_____
			_____
			_____

January 2025

6 Monday	7 Tuesday	8 Wednesday
_____	_____	_____
_____	_____	_____
_____	_____	_____
_____	_____	_____
_____	_____	_____
_____	_____	_____
_____	_____	_____
_____	_____	_____
_____	_____	_____
_____	_____	_____
_____	_____	_____
_____	_____	_____
_____	_____	_____
○ _____	○ _____	○ _____
○ _____	○ _____	○ _____
○ _____	○ _____	○ _____
○ _____	○ _____	○ _____
○ _____	○ _____	○ _____
○ _____	○ _____	○ _____
○ _____	○ _____	○ _____
○ _____	○ _____	○ _____
○ _____	○ _____	○ _____

Important as fuck

_____

_____

_____

Fucking grateful for…

_____

_____

_____

Ka-POW, bitch! Time to bring that badass energy.

9 Thursday	10 Friday	11 Saturday
_____	_____	_____
_____	_____	_____
_____	_____	_____
_____	_____	_____
_____	_____	_____
_____	_____	_____
_____	_____	○ _____
_____	_____	○ _____
_____	_____	○ _____

12 Sunday

_____	_____	_____
_____	_____	_____
○ _____	○ _____	_____
○ _____	○ _____	_____
○ _____	○ _____	_____
○ _____	○ _____	_____
○ _____	○ _____	_____
○ _____	○ _____	_____
○ _____	○ _____	○ _____
○ _____	○ _____	○ _____
○ _____	○ _____	○ _____

Notes and shit

_____

_____

_____

January 2025

13 Monday   14 Tuesday   15 Wednesday

_____   _____   _____
_____   _____   _____
_____   _____   _____
_____   _____   _____
_____   _____   _____
_____   _____   _____
_____   _____   _____
_____   _____   _____
_____   _____   _____
_____   _____   _____

○ _____   ○ _____   ○ _____
○ _____   ○ _____   ○ _____
○ _____   ○ _____   ○ _____
○ _____   ○ _____   ○ _____
○ _____   ○ _____   ○ _____
○ _____   ○ _____   ○ _____
○ _____   ○ _____   ○ _____
○ _____   ○ _____   ○ _____
○ _____   ○ _____   ○ _____

Important as fuck   Fucking grateful for...

_____   _____
_____   _____
_____   _____

You are a fucking star. But keep reaching for the stars anyway. Because you're not a lazy star. #fuckingstargoals

16 Thursday

_____
_____
_____
_____
_____
_____
_____
_____
_____
_____
_____
_____
○ _____
○ _____
○ _____
○ _____
○ _____
○ _____
○ _____
○ _____
○ _____

17 Friday

_____
_____
_____
_____
_____
_____
_____
_____
_____
_____
_____
○ _____
○ _____
○ _____
○ _____
○ _____
○ _____
○ _____
○ _____
○ _____

18 Saturday

_____
_____
_____
_____
_____
_____
○ _____
○ _____
○ _____

19 Sunday

_____
_____
_____
_____
_____
○ _____
○ _____
○ _____

Notes and shit

_____
_____
_____

January 2025

20 Monday
Martin Luther King Jr. Day (US),
Inauguration Day (US)

21 Tuesday

22 Wednesday

_____
_____
_____
_____
_____
_____
_____
_____
_____
_____
_____
_____

- ○ _____
- ○ _____
- ○ _____
- ○ _____
- ○ _____
- ○ _____
- ○ _____
- ○ _____
- ○ _____

Important as fuck

_____
_____
_____

Fucking grateful for...

_____
_____
_____

Take a deep breath, check your nails, and make shit happen

23 Thursday

_____
_____
_____
_____
_____
_____
_____
_____
_____
_____
_____
_____
○ _____
○ _____
○ _____
○ _____
○ _____
○ _____
○ _____
○ _____
○ _____

24 Friday

_____
_____
_____
_____
_____
_____
_____
_____
_____
_____
○ _____
○ _____
○ _____
○ _____
○ _____
○ _____
○ _____
○ _____
○ _____

25 Saturday

_____
_____
_____
_____
_____
_____
○ _____
○ _____
○ _____

26 Sunday

_____
_____
_____
_____
_____
_____
○ _____
○ _____
○ _____

Notes and shit

_____
_____
_____

January-February 2025

27 Monday
Australia Day (AU)

28 Tuesday

29 Wednesday
Chinese New Year

Important as fuck

Fucking grateful for...

Your eyes sparkle with wisdom, curiosity, and mischief. What the fuck are you up to, bitch?

30 Thursday	31 Friday	1 Saturday
_____	_____	_____
_____	_____	_____
_____	_____	_____
_____	_____	_____
_____	_____	_____
_____	_____	_____
_____	_____	○ _____
_____	_____	○ _____
_____	_____	○ _____

2 Sunday
Groundhog Day (US, CA)

○ _____	○ _____	_____
○ _____	○ _____	_____
○ _____	○ _____	_____
○ _____	○ _____	_____
○ _____	○ _____	_____
○ _____	○ _____	_____
○ _____	○ _____	○ _____
○ _____	○ _____	○ _____
○ _____	○ _____	○ _____

Notes and shit

_____
_____
_____

February 2025

Sunday	Monday	Tuesday	Wednesday
JANUARY 2025 S M T W T F S 　　　　1 2 3 4 5 6 7 8 9 10 11 12 13 14 15 16 17 18 19 20 21 22 23 24 25 26 27 28 29 30 31	**MARCH 2025** S M T W T F S 　　　　　　1 2 3 4 5 6 7 8 9 10 11 12 13 14 15 16 17 18 19 20 21 22 23 24 25 26 27 28 29 30 31		
2 Groundhog Day (US, CA)	3	4	5
9	10	11	12
16	17 Presidents' Day (US)	18	19
23	24	25	26

You are even stronger than your fucking language

Thursday	Friday	Saturday	Important shit
		1	_____
6	7	8	_____
13	14 Valentine's Day	15	_____
20	21	22	_____
27	28 Ramadan begins		_____

February 2025

3 Monday

_____
_____
_____
_____
_____
_____
_____
_____
_____
_____
_____
_____
_____
○ _____
○ _____
○ _____
○ _____
○ _____
○ _____
○ _____
○ _____
○ _____

4 Tuesday

_____
_____
_____
_____
_____
_____
_____
_____
_____
_____
_____
_____
_____
○ _____
○ _____
○ _____
○ _____
○ _____
○ _____
○ _____
○ _____
○ _____

5 Wednesday

_____
_____
_____
_____
_____
_____
_____
_____
_____
_____
_____
_____
_____
○ _____
○ _____
○ _____
○ _____
○ _____
○ _____
○ _____
○ _____
○ _____

Important as fuck

_____
_____
_____

Fucking grateful for...

_____
_____
_____

If swear words are "colorful language," maybe add "Fucking Artist" to your profiles?

6 Thursday

_____
_____
_____
_____
_____
_____
_____
_____
_____
_____
_____

- ○ _____
- ○ _____
- ○ _____
- ○ _____
- ○ _____
- ○ _____
- ○ _____
- ○ _____
- ○ _____

7 Friday

_____
_____
_____
_____
_____
_____
_____
_____
_____
_____
_____

- ○ _____
- ○ _____
- ○ _____
- ○ _____
- ○ _____
- ○ _____
- ○ _____
- ○ _____
- ○ _____

8 Saturday

_____
_____
_____
_____
_____

- ○ _____
- ○ _____
- ○ _____

9 Sunday

_____
_____
_____
_____

- ○ _____
- ○ _____
- ○ _____

Notes and shit

_____
_____
_____

February 2025

10 Monday

_____
_____
_____
_____
_____
_____
_____
_____
_____
_____
_____
_____
_____

○ _____
○ _____
○ _____
○ _____
○ _____
○ _____
○ _____
○ _____
○ _____

11 Tuesday

_____
_____
_____
_____
_____
_____
_____
_____
_____
_____
_____
_____
_____

○ _____
○ _____
○ _____
○ _____
○ _____
○ _____
○ _____
○ _____
○ _____

12 Wednesday

_____
_____
_____
_____
_____
_____
_____
_____
_____
_____
_____
_____
_____

○ _____
○ _____
○ _____
○ _____
○ _____
○ _____
○ _____
○ _____
○ _____

Important as fuck

_____
_____
_____

Fucking grateful for...

_____
_____
_____

Be your own valentine. Break up with negative thoughts, bitch.

13 Thursday

_____
_____
_____
_____
_____
_____
_____
_____
_____
_____
_____
_____

○ _____
○ _____
○ _____
○ _____
○ _____
○ _____
○ _____
○ _____
○ _____

14 Friday
Valentine's Day

_____
_____
_____
_____
_____
_____
_____
_____
_____
_____

○ _____
○ _____
○ _____
○ _____
○ _____
○ _____
○ _____
○ _____
○ _____

15 Saturday

_____
_____
_____
_____
_____
○ _____
○ _____
○ _____

16 Sunday

_____
_____
_____
_____
_____
○ _____
○ _____
○ _____

Notes and shit

_____
_____
_____

February 2025

17 Monday
Presidents' Day (US)

_____
_____
_____
_____
_____
_____
_____
_____
_____
_____
_____
_____
_____
- ○ _____
- ○ _____
- ○ _____
- ○ _____
- ○ _____
- ○ _____
- ○ _____
- ○ _____
- ○ _____

18 Tuesday

_____
_____
_____
_____
_____
_____
_____
_____
_____
_____
_____
_____
_____
- ○ _____
- ○ _____
- ○ _____
- ○ _____
- ○ _____
- ○ _____
- ○ _____
- ○ _____
- ○ _____

19 Wednesday

_____
_____
_____
_____
_____
_____
_____
_____
_____
_____
_____
_____
_____
- ○ _____
- ○ _____
- ○ _____
- ○ _____
- ○ _____
- ○ _____
- ○ _____
- ○ _____
- ○ _____

Important as fuck

_____
_____
_____

Fucking grateful for...

_____
_____
_____

You fucking rock. Please don't worry about assholes. I'll take care of them. xoxo Karma

20 Thursday

21 Friday

22 Saturday

○
○
○

23 Sunday

○
○
○
○
○
○
○
○
○

○
○
○
○
○
○
○
○
○

○
○
○

Notes and shit

February-March 2025

24 Monday	25 Tuesday	26 Wednesday
_____	_____	_____
_____	_____	_____
_____	_____	_____
_____	_____	_____
_____	_____	_____
_____	_____	_____
_____	_____	_____
_____	_____	_____
_____	_____	_____
_____	_____	_____
_____	_____	_____
_____	_____	_____
○ _____	○ _____	○ _____
○ _____	○ _____	○ _____
○ _____	○ _____	○ _____
○ _____	○ _____	○ _____
○ _____	○ _____	○ _____
○ _____	○ _____	○ _____
○ _____	○ _____	○ _____
○ _____	○ _____	○ _____
○ _____	○ _____	○ _____

Important as fuck

_____
_____
_____

Fucking grateful for...

_____
_____
_____

What's your beauty secret? Drink water and glow like fucking sunshine?

27 Thursday

28 Friday
Ramadan begins

1 Saturday

- ○
- ○
- ○

2 Sunday

- ○
- ○
- ○
- ○
- ○
- ○
- ○
- ○
- ○

- ○
- ○
- ○
- ○
- ○
- ○
- ○
- ○
- ○

- ○
- ○
- ○

Notes and shit

March 2025

Sunday	Monday	Tuesday	Wednesday
FEBRUARY 2025 S M T W T F S 　　　　　　1 2 3 4 5 6 7 8 9 10 11 12 13 14 15 16 17 18 19 20 21 22 23 24 25 26 27 28	**APRIL 2025** S M T W T F S 　　1 2 3 4 5 6 7 8 9 10 11 12 13 14 15 16 17 18 19 20 21 22 23 24 25 26 27 28 29 30		
2	3	4 Mardi Gras	5 Ash Wednesday
9 Daylight Saving Time begins (US, CA)	10	11	12
16	17 St. Patrick's Day	18	19
23	24	25	26
30 Mother's Day (UK), Eid al-Fitr begins	31		

Waking up and kicking ass again today? That's so you.

Thursday	Friday	Saturday	Important shit
		1	_____
			_____
			_____
6	7	8	_____
			_____
		International Women's Day	_____
13	14	15	_____
			_____
Purim begins			_____
20	21	22	_____
			_____
Spring begins (Northern Hemisphere)			_____
27	28	29	_____
			_____
			_____
			_____
			_____
			_____

March 2025

3 Monday

4 Tuesday
Mardi Gras

5 Wednesday
Ash Wednesday

_____
_____
_____
_____
_____
_____
_____
_____
_____
_____
_____
_____

○ _____
○ _____
○ _____
○ _____
○ _____
○ _____
○ _____
○ _____
○ _____

Important as fuck

_____
_____
_____

Fucking grateful for...

_____
_____
_____

You will fuck up. We all do. And then you will rise up like a fucking phoenix. But maybe do something nice for yourself first. Grab a coffee or watch a show or something. Then do the phoenix-y thing.

6 Thursday

_____
_____
_____
_____
_____
_____
_____
_____
_____
_____
_____

- _____
- _____
- _____
- _____
- _____
- _____
- _____
- _____
- _____

7 Friday

_____
_____
_____
_____
_____
_____
_____
_____
_____

- _____
- _____
- _____
- _____
- _____
- _____
- _____
- _____
- _____

8 Saturday
International Women's Day

_____
_____
_____
_____
_____
- _____
- _____
- _____

9 Sunday
Daylight Saving Time begins (US, CA)

_____
_____
_____
_____
- _____
- _____
- _____

Notes and shit

_____
_____
_____

March 2025

10 Monday

11 Tuesday

12 Wednesday

○ _____
○ _____
○ _____
○ _____
○ _____
○ _____
○ _____
○ _____
○ _____

Important as fuck

_____
_____
_____

Fucking grateful for...

_____
_____
_____

Choosing your happiness over someone else's fucking drama? Bold choice.

13 Thursday
Purim begins

_____
_____
_____
_____
_____
_____
_____
_____
_____
_____
_____
_____
_____

○ _____
○ _____
○ _____
○ _____
○ _____
○ _____
○ _____
○ _____
○ _____

14 Friday

_____
_____
_____
_____
_____
_____
_____
_____
_____
_____
_____

○ _____
○ _____
○ _____
○ _____
○ _____
○ _____
○ _____
○ _____
○ _____

15 Saturday

_____
_____
_____
_____
_____
_____
○ _____
○ _____
○ _____

16 Sunday

_____
_____
_____
_____
_____
○ _____
○ _____
○ _____

Notes and shit

_____
_____
_____

March 2025

17 Monday
St. Patrick's Day

18 Tuesday

19 Wednesday

Important as fuck

Fucking grateful for...

In honor of St. Patrick's Day, all "colorful" language will be green. F♣ck It!

20 Thursday
Spring begins (Northern Hemisphere)

21 Friday

22 Saturday

23 Sunday

Notes and shit

March 2025

24 Monday	25 Tuesday	26 Wednesday

Important as fuck

Fucking grateful for…

Don't take shit from anyone. Especially not yourself!

27 Thursday

_____
_____
_____
_____
_____
_____
_____
_____
_____
_____
_____
_____
_____

○ _____
○ _____
○ _____
○ _____
○ _____
○ _____
○ _____
○ _____
○ _____

28 Friday

_____
_____
_____
_____
_____
_____
_____
_____
_____
_____
_____

○ _____
○ _____
○ _____
○ _____
○ _____
○ _____
○ _____
○ _____
○ _____

29 Saturday

_____
_____
_____
_____
_____
_____
○ _____
○ _____
○ _____

30 Sunday
Mother's Day (UK), Eid al-Fitr begins

_____
_____
_____
_____
_____
○ _____
○ _____
○ _____

Notes and shit

_____
_____
_____

April 2025

Sunday	Monday	Tuesday	Wednesday
MARCH 2025 S M T W T F S 　　　　　　1 2 3 4 5 6 7 8 9 10 11 12 13 14 15 16 17 18 19 20 21 22 23 24 25 26 27 28 29 30 31	**MAY 2025** S M T W T F S 　　　　1 2 3 4 5 6 7 8 9 10 11 12 13 14 15 16 17 18 19 20 21 22 23 24 25 26 27 28 29 30 31	1 April Fools' Day	2
6	7	8	9
13 Palm Sunday	14	15 Tax Day (US)	16
20 Easter	21 Easter Monday	22 Earth Day	23
27	28	29	30

You express yourself beautifully. With your eyes, your smile, your words... and your middle finger.

Thursday	Friday	Saturday	Important shit
3	4	5	_____ _____ _____ _____
10	11	12 Passover begins	_____ _____ _____ _____
17	18 Good Friday	19	_____ _____ _____ _____
24	25 Anzac Day (AU)	26	_____ _____ _____ _____
			_____ _____ _____ _____ _____

March-April 2025

31 Monday

1 Tuesday
April Fools' Day

2 Wednesday

_____

○
○
○
○
○
○
○
○
○

Important as fuck

_____
_____
_____

Fucking grateful for...

_____
_____
_____

You're amazing, beautiful, confident, delightful, empathetic, friendly, generous, happy, intelligent, joyful, kind ... Damn, describing you is easy. Doing it without swearing is the hard part!

3 Thursday

_____
_____
_____
_____
_____
_____
_____
_____
_____
_____
_____

○ _____
○ _____
○ _____
○ _____
○ _____
○ _____
○ _____
○ _____
○ _____

4 Friday

_____
_____
_____
_____
_____
_____
_____

○ _____
○ _____
○ _____
○ _____
○ _____
○ _____
○ _____
○ _____
○ _____

5 Saturday

_____
_____
_____
_____
_____
○ _____
○ _____
○ _____

6 Sunday

_____
_____
_____
_____
_____
_____
○ _____
○ _____
○ _____

Notes and shit

_____
_____
_____

April 2025

7 Monday   8 Tuesday   9 Wednesday

Important as fuck

Fucking grateful for...

You attract good shit and block bullshit as effortlessly as raising your middle finger

10 Thursday

_____
_____
_____
_____
_____
_____
_____
_____
_____
_____
_____
_____

○ _____
○ _____
○ _____
○ _____
○ _____
○ _____
○ _____
○ _____
○ _____

11 Friday

_____
_____
_____
_____
_____
_____
_____

○ _____
○ _____
○ _____
○ _____
○ _____
○ _____
○ _____
○ _____
○ _____

12 Saturday
Passover begins

_____
_____
_____
_____
_____

○ _____
○ _____
○ _____

13 Sunday
Palm Sunday

_____
_____
_____
_____
_____

○ _____
○ _____
○ _____

Notes and shit

_____
_____
_____

April 2025

14 Monday	15 Tuesday	16 Wednesday
	Tax Day (US)	

○
○
○
○
○
○
○
○
○

Important as fuck

Fucking grateful for...

Swearing _is_ your love language

17 Thursday

18 Friday
Good Friday

19 Saturday

○
○
○

20 Sunday
Easter

○
○
○
○
○
○
○
○
○

○
○
○
○
○
○
○
○
○

○
○
○

Notes and shit

April 2025

21 Monday
Easter Monday

22 Tuesday
Earth Day

23 Wednesday

Important as fuck

Fucking grateful for…

You have a long year of kicking ass ahead of you. So, stay stretchy, bitch. You don't want to pull a muscle.

24 Thursday

_____
_____
_____
_____
_____
_____
_____
_____
_____
_____
_____
_____

○ _____
○ _____
○ _____
○ _____
○ _____
○ _____
○ _____
○ _____
○ _____

25 Friday
Anzac Day (AU)

_____
_____
_____
_____
_____
_____
_____
_____
_____
_____
_____

○ _____
○ _____
○ _____
○ _____
○ _____
○ _____
○ _____
○ _____
○ _____

26 Saturday

_____
_____
_____
_____
_____
○ _____
○ _____
○ _____

27 Sunday

_____
_____
_____
_____
_____
_____
○ _____
○ _____
○ _____

Notes and shit

_____
_____
_____

May 2025

Sunday	Monday	Tuesday	Wednesday
APRIL 2025 S M T W T F S 1 2 3 4 5 6 7 8 9 10 11 12 13 14 15 16 17 18 19 20 21 22 23 24 25 26 27 28 29 30	**JUNE 2025** S M T W T F S 1 2 3 4 5 6 7 8 9 10 11 12 13 14 15 16 17 18 19 20 21 22 23 24 25 26 27 28 29 30		
4	5 Cinco de Mayo (US), Early May Bank Holiday (UK)	6	7
11 Mother's Day (US, CA, AU)	12	13	14
18	19 Victoria Day (CA)	20	21
25	26 Memorial Day (US), Spring Bank Holiday (UK)	27	28

Play like a girl, win like a fucking boss

Thursday	Friday	Saturday	Important shit
1	2	3	_____ _____ _____ _____
8	9	10	_____ _____ _____ _____
15	16	17 Armed Forces Day (US)	_____ _____ _____ _____
22	23	24	_____ _____ _____ _____
29	30	31	_____ _____ _____ _____

April-May 2025

28 Monday | 29 Tuesday | 30 Wednesday

_____
_____
_____
_____
_____
_____
_____
_____
_____
_____
_____
_____

○ _____
○ _____
○ _____
○ _____
○ _____
○ _____
○ _____
○ _____
○ _____

Important as fuck

_____
_____
_____

Fucking grateful for...

_____
_____
_____

Doubts can pile up like clutter. But at least you don't have to stress about what to get rid of. All that shit is TRASH.

1 Thursday	2 Friday	3 Saturday
_____	_____	_____
_____	_____	_____
_____	_____	_____
_____	_____	_____
_____	_____	_____
_____	_____	_____
_____	_____	○ _____
_____	_____	○ _____
_____	_____	○ _____

4 Sunday

_____

_____

○ _____

○ _____

○ Thursday list:

- ○ _____
- ○ _____
- ○ _____
- ○ _____
- ○ _____
- ○ _____
- ○ _____
- ○ _____
- ○ _____

Friday list:

- ○ _____
- ○ _____
- ○ _____
- ○ _____
- ○ _____
- ○ _____
- ○ _____
- ○ _____
- ○ _____

Notes and shit

_____

_____

_____

May 2025

5 Monday
Cinco de Mayo (US), Early May Bank
Holiday (UK)

_____
_____
_____
_____
_____
_____
_____
_____
_____
_____
_____
○ _____
○ _____
○ _____
○ _____
○ _____
○ _____
○ _____
○ _____
○ _____

6 Tuesday

_____
_____
_____
_____
_____
_____
_____
_____
_____
_____
_____
○ _____
○ _____
○ _____
○ _____
○ _____
○ _____
○ _____
○ _____
○ _____

7 Wednesday

_____
_____
_____
_____
_____
_____
_____
_____
_____
_____
_____
○ _____
○ _____
○ _____
○ _____
○ _____
○ _____
○ _____
○ _____
○ _____

Important as fuck

_____
_____
_____

Fucking grateful for…

_____
_____
_____

Asking for help is a sign of strength. Get your reps in, bitch.

8 Thursday

_____
_____
_____
_____
_____
_____
_____
_____
_____
_____
_____
_____
_____

○ _____
○ _____
○ _____
○ _____
○ _____
○ _____
○ _____
○ _____
○ _____

9 Friday

_____
_____
_____
_____
_____
_____
_____
_____

○ _____
○ _____
○ _____
○ _____
○ _____
○ _____
○ _____
○ _____
○ _____

10 Saturday

_____
_____
_____
_____
_____

○ _____
○ _____
○ _____

11 Sunday
Mother's Day (US, CA, AU)

_____
_____
_____
_____
_____
_____

○ _____
○ _____
○ _____

Notes and shit

_____
_____
_____

May 2025

12 Monday	13 Tuesday	14 Wednesday
_____	_____	_____
_____	_____	_____
_____	_____	_____
_____	_____	_____
_____	_____	_____
_____	_____	_____
_____	_____	_____
_____	_____	_____
_____	_____	_____
_____	_____	_____
_____	_____	_____
_____	_____	_____
○ _____	○ _____	○ _____
○ _____	○ _____	○ _____
○ _____	○ _____	○ _____
○ _____	○ _____	○ _____
○ _____	○ _____	○ _____
○ _____	○ _____	○ _____
○ _____	○ _____	○ _____
○ _____	○ _____	○ _____
○ _____	○ _____	○ _____

Important as fuck

_____

_____

_____

Fucking grateful for…

_____

_____

_____

Your opinions, like your heart, are fucking gold

15 Thursday

_____
_____
_____
_____
_____
_____
_____
_____
_____
_____
_____
_____
_____

○ _____
○ _____
○ _____
○ _____
○ _____
○ _____
○ _____
○ _____
○ _____

16 Friday

_____
_____
_____
_____
_____
_____
_____
_____
_____
_____
_____
_____
_____

○ _____
○ _____
○ _____
○ _____
○ _____
○ _____
○ _____
○ _____
○ _____

17 Saturday
Armed Forces Day (US)

_____
_____
_____
_____
_____
○ _____
○ _____
○ _____

18 Sunday

_____
_____
_____
_____
_____
_____
○ _____
○ _____
○ _____

Notes and shit

_____
_____
_____

May 2025

19 Monday
Victoria Day (CA)

20 Tuesday

21 Wednesday

_____
_____
_____
_____
_____
_____
_____
_____
_____
_____
_____
_____

- ○ _____
- ○ _____
- ○ _____
- ○ _____
- ○ _____
- ○ _____
- ○ _____
- ○ _____
- ○ _____

Important as fuck

_____
_____
_____

Fucking grateful for...

_____
_____
_____

Want to master the art of saying "No"? Easy. Use bold, colorful language, like "Hell No," "Are you fucking kidding me?," and "Fuck off." And voila! You've got a masterpiece.

22 Thursday

_____
_____
_____
_____
_____
_____
_____
_____
_____
_____
_____
_____
_____
_____

○ _____
○ _____
○ _____
○ _____
○ _____
○ _____
○ _____
○ _____
○ _____

23 Friday

_____
_____
_____
_____
_____
_____
_____
_____
_____
_____
_____
_____

○ _____
○ _____
○ _____
○ _____
○ _____
○ _____
○ _____
○ _____
○ _____

24 Saturday

_____
_____
_____
_____
_____
_____

○ _____
○ _____
○ _____

25 Sunday

_____
_____
_____
_____
_____
_____

○ _____
○ _____
○ _____

Notes and shit

_____
_____
_____

May-June 2025

26 Monday
Memorial Day (US), Spring Bank
Holiday (UK)

27 Tuesday

28 Wednesday

Important as fuck

Fucking grateful for…

Say "Sayonara" to imposter syndrome, that toxic bitch

29 Thursday

○ _____
○ _____
○ _____
○ _____
○ _____
○ _____
○ _____
○ _____
○ _____

30 Friday

○ _____
○ _____
○ _____
○ _____
○ _____
○ _____
○ _____
○ _____
○ _____

31 Saturday

○ _____
○ _____
○ _____

1 Sunday
Shavuot begins

○ _____
○ _____
○ _____

Notes and shit

June 2025

Sunday	Monday	Tuesday	Wednesday
1 Shavuot begins	2	3	4
8	9	10	11
15 Father's Day (US, UK, CA)	16	17	18
22	23	24	25
29	30		

You float over fuckery like a badass butterfly

Thursday	Friday	Saturday	Important shit
5	6 Eid al-Adha begins	7	_____ _____ _____ _____
12	13	14 Flag Day (US)	_____ _____ _____ _____
19 Juneteenth (US)	20 Summer begins (Northern Hemisphere)	21 King's Birthday (UK), National Indigenous Peoples Day (CA)	_____ _____ _____ _____
26 Muharram begins	27	28	_____ _____ _____ _____

MAY 2025

S	M	T	W	T	F	S
				1	2	3
4	5	6	7	8	9	10
11	12	13	14	15	16	17
18	19	20	21	22	23	24
25	26	27	28	29	30	31

JULY 2025

S	M	T	W	T	F	S
		1	2	3	4	5
6	7	8	9	10	11	12
13	14	15	16	17	18	19
20	21	22	23	24	25	26
27	28	29	30	31		

June 2025

2 Monday

3 Tuesday

4 Wednesday

○ _____
○ _____
○ _____
○ _____
○ _____
○ _____
○ _____
○ _____
○ _____

○ _____
○ _____
○ _____
○ _____
○ _____
○ _____
○ _____
○ _____
○ _____

○ _____
○ _____
○ _____
○ _____
○ _____
○ _____
○ _____
○ _____
○ _____

Important as fuck

_____
_____
_____

Fucking grateful for…

_____
_____
_____

Everything you need to succeed is within you. You're like a beautiful, walking, talking purse full of useful shit.

5 Thursday

_____
_____
_____
_____
_____
_____
_____
_____
_____
_____
_____
_____
○ _____
○ _____
○ _____
○ _____
○ _____
○ _____
○ _____
○ _____
○ _____

6 Friday
Eid al-Adha begins

_____
_____
_____
_____
_____
_____
_____
_____
_____
_____
_____
_____
○ _____
○ _____
○ _____
○ _____
○ _____
○ _____
○ _____
○ _____
○ _____

7 Saturday

_____
_____
_____
_____
_____
○ _____
○ _____
○ _____

8 Sunday

_____
_____
_____
_____
○ _____
○ _____
○ _____

Notes and shit

_____
_____
_____

June 2025

9 Monday   10 Tuesday   11 Wednesday

Important as fuck

Fucking grateful for...

You even brighten up Mondays, you awesome bitch

12 Thursday

○ ——————
○ ——————
○ ——————
○ ——————
○ ——————
○ ——————
○ ——————
○ ——————
○ ——————

13 Friday

○ ——————
○ ——————
○ ——————
○ ——————
○ ——————
○ ——————
○ ——————
○ ——————
○ ——————

14 Saturday
Flag Day (US)

○ ——————
○ ——————
○ ——————

15 Sunday
Father's Day (US, UK, CA)

○ ——————
○ ——————
○ ——————

Notes and shit

June 2025

16 Monday	17 Tuesday	18 Wednesday

Important as fuck

Fucking grateful for...

Being yourself is the best thing for you. But you're also setting a great example for aspiring bitches everywhere.

19 Thursday
Juneteenth (US)

20 Friday
Summer begins (Northern Hemisphere)

21 Saturday
King's Birthday (UK), National Indigenous Peoples Day (CA)

○
○
○

22 Sunday

○
○
○

Notes and shit

June 2025

23 Monday   24 Tuesday   25 Wednesday

Important as fuck

Fucking grateful for…

Keep your friends close and your enemies... can go fuck themselves

26 Thursday
Muharram begins

_____
_____
_____
_____
_____
_____
_____
_____
_____
_____
_____
_____

- ○ _____
- ○ _____
- ○ _____
- ○ _____
- ○ _____
- ○ _____
- ○ _____
- ○ _____
- ○ _____

27 Friday

_____
_____
_____
_____
_____
_____
_____
_____
_____
_____
_____

- ○ _____
- ○ _____
- ○ _____
- ○ _____
- ○ _____
- ○ _____
- ○ _____
- ○ _____
- ○ _____

28 Saturday

_____
_____
_____
_____
- ○ _____
- ○ _____
- ○ _____

29 Sunday

_____
_____
_____
_____
_____
- ○ _____
- ○ _____
- ○ _____

Notes and shit

_____
_____
_____

July 2025

Sunday	Monday	Tuesday	Wednesday
JUNE 2025 S M T W T F S 1 2 3 4 5 6 7 8 9 10 11 12 13 14 15 16 17 18 19 20 21 22 23 24 25 26 27 28 29 30	**AUGUST 2025** S M T W T F S 1 2 3 4 5 6 7 8 9 10 11 12 13 14 15 16 17 18 19 20 21 22 23 24 25 26 27 28 29 30 31	1 Canada Day (CA)	2
6	7	8	9
13	14	15	16
20	21	22	23
27	28	29	30

Rock what you got, you fabulous bitch

Thursday	Friday	Saturday	Important shit
3	4 Independence Day (US)	5	_____ _____ _____
10	11	12	_____ _____ _____
17	18	19	_____ _____ _____
24	25	26	_____ _____ _____
31			_____ _____ _____

June-July 2025

30 Monday

1 Tuesday
Canada Day (CA)

2 Wednesday

_____
_____
_____
_____
_____
_____
_____
_____
_____
_____
_____
_____

○ _____
○ _____
○ _____
○ _____
○ _____
○ _____
○ _____
○ _____
○ _____

Important as fuck

_____
_____
_____

Fucking grateful for...

_____
_____
_____

Overwhelmed? Chuck some shit in the fuck-it bucket. Perfection? Fuck it. What "they" say? Fuck it. Now you try it :)

3 Thursday

_____
_____
_____
_____
_____
_____
_____
_____
_____
_____
_____
○ _____
○ _____
○ _____
○ _____
○ _____
○ _____
○ _____
○ _____
○ _____

4 Friday
Independence Day (US)

_____
_____
_____
_____
_____
_____
_____
_____
_____
_____
_____
○ _____
○ _____
○ _____
○ _____
○ _____
○ _____
○ _____
○ _____
○ _____

5 Saturday

_____
_____
_____
_____
_____
○ _____
○ _____
○ _____

6 Sunday

_____
_____
_____
_____
_____
○ _____
○ _____
○ _____

Notes and shit

_____
_____
_____

July 2025

7 Monday   8 Tuesday   9 Wednesday

Important as fuck

Fucking grateful for...

You do amazing things every fucking day. And some days, just getting out of bed will feel like an amazing accomplishment. Every win counts, bitch.

10 Thursday

11 Friday

12 Saturday

13 Sunday

Notes and shit

July 2025

14 Monday

15 Tuesday

16 Wednesday

Important as fuck

Fucking grateful for...

Plan for the day: Wake up. Spread fucking joy. Repeat.

17 Thursday

_____
_____
_____
_____
_____
_____
_____
_____
_____
_____
_____
_____

- ○ _____
- ○ _____
- ○ _____
- ○ _____
- ○ _____
- ○ _____
- ○ _____
- ○ _____
- ○ _____

18 Friday

_____
_____
_____
_____
_____
_____
_____
_____
_____
_____
_____
_____

- ○ _____
- ○ _____
- ○ _____
- ○ _____
- ○ _____
- ○ _____
- ○ _____
- ○ _____
- ○ _____

19 Saturday

_____
_____
_____
_____
_____
- ○ _____
- ○ _____
- ○ _____

20 Sunday

_____
_____
_____
_____
_____
- ○ _____
- ○ _____
- ○ _____

Notes and shit

_____
_____
_____

July 2025

21 Monday   22 Tuesday   23 Wednesday

_____   _____   _____
_____   _____   _____
_____   _____   _____
_____   _____   _____
_____   _____   _____
_____   _____   _____
_____   _____   _____
_____   _____   _____
_____   _____   _____
_____   _____   _____
_____   _____   _____
_____   _____   _____

- [ ] _____   - [ ] _____   - [ ] _____
- [ ] _____   - [ ] _____   - [ ] _____
- [ ] _____   - [ ] _____   - [ ] _____
- [ ] _____   - [ ] _____   - [ ] _____
- [ ] _____   - [ ] _____   - [ ] _____
- [ ] _____   - [ ] _____   - [ ] _____
- [ ] _____   - [ ] _____   - [ ] _____
- [ ] _____   - [ ] _____   - [ ] _____
- [ ] _____   - [ ] _____   - [ ] _____

Important as fuck

_____

_____

_____

Fucking grateful for...

_____

_____

_____

look at you being talented, kind and beautiful. That's some badass multitasking, bitch.

24 Thursday	25 Friday	26 Saturday

27 Sunday

Notes and shit

July-August 2025

28 Monday	29 Tuesday	30 Wednesday

○ _____
○ _____
○ _____
○ _____
○ _____
○ _____
○ _____
○ _____
○ _____

Important as fuck

_____
_____
_____

Fucking grateful for...

_____
_____
_____

Ignore haters who try to shit on your success. It's just their little hater thing. like some kind of stupid "crapbooking" hobby.

31 Thursday

_____
_____
_____
_____
_____
_____
_____
_____
_____
_____
_____
_____

○ _____
○ _____
○ _____
○ _____
○ _____
○ _____
○ _____
○ _____
○ _____

1 Friday

_____
_____
_____
_____
_____
_____
_____
_____
_____
_____
_____
_____

○ _____
○ _____
○ _____
○ _____
○ _____
○ _____
○ _____
○ _____
○ _____

2 Saturday

_____
_____
_____
_____
_____
_____
○ _____
○ _____
○ _____

3 Sunday

_____
_____
_____
_____
_____
○ _____
○ _____
○ _____

Notes and shit

_____
_____
_____

August 2025

Sunday	Monday	Tuesday	Wednesday
JULY 2025 S M T W T F S 　 　 1 2 3 4 5 6 7 8 9 10 11 12 13 14 15 16 17 18 19 20 21 22 23 24 25 26 27 28 29 30 31	**SEPTEMBER 2025** S M T W T F S 　 1 2 3 4 5 6 7 8 9 10 11 12 13 14 15 16 17 18 19 20 21 22 23 24 25 26 27 28 29 30		
3	4 Civic Holiday (CA)	5	6
10	11	12	13
17	18	19	20
24	25 Summer Bank Holiday (UK)	26	27
31			

Your road to fucking happiness is paved with good intentions and even better actions

Thursday	Friday	Saturday	Important shit
	1	2	_____
7	8	9	_____
14	15	16	_____
21	22	23	_____
28	29	30	_____
			_____

August 2025

4 Monday
Civic Holiday (CA)

_____
_____
_____
_____
_____
_____
_____
_____
_____
_____
_____

○ _____
○ _____
○ _____
○ _____
○ _____
○ _____
○ _____
○ _____
○ _____

5 Tuesday

_____
_____
_____
_____
_____
_____
_____
_____
_____
_____
_____

○ _____
○ _____
○ _____
○ _____
○ _____
○ _____
○ _____
○ _____
○ _____

6 Wednesday

_____
_____
_____
_____
_____
_____
_____
_____
_____
_____
_____

○ _____
○ _____
○ _____
○ _____
○ _____
○ _____
○ _____
○ _____
○ _____

Important as fuck
_____
_____

Fucking grateful for…
_____
_____

You are a ray of fucking sunshine no matter how much shade assholes try to throw

7 Thursday

_____
_____
_____
_____
_____
_____
_____
_____
_____
_____
_____
_____

○ _____
○ _____
○ _____
○ _____
○ _____
○ _____
○ _____
○ _____
○ _____

8 Friday

_____
_____
_____
_____
_____
_____
_____
_____
_____
_____
_____

○ _____
○ _____
○ _____
○ _____
○ _____
○ _____
○ _____
○ _____
○ _____

9 Saturday

_____
_____
_____
_____
_____
○ _____
○ _____
○ _____

10 Sunday

_____
_____
_____
_____
_____
_____
○ _____
○ _____
○ _____

Notes and shit

_____
_____
_____

August 2025

11 Monday   12 Tuesday   13 Wednesday

Important as fuck

Fucking grateful for...

You're too grounded to give a flying fuck

14 Thursday

_____
_____
_____
_____
_____
_____
_____
_____
_____
_____
_____
_____
○ _____
○ _____
○ _____
○ _____
○ _____
○ _____
○ _____
○ _____
○ _____

15 Friday

_____
_____
_____
_____
_____
_____
_____
_____
_____
_____
○ _____
○ _____
○ _____
○ _____
○ _____
○ _____
○ _____
○ _____
○ _____

16 Saturday

_____
_____
_____
_____
_____
_____
○ _____
○ _____
○ _____

17 Sunday

_____
_____
_____
_____
_____
_____
○ _____
○ _____
○ _____

Notes and shit

_____
_____
_____

August 2025

18 Monday	19 Tuesday	20 Wednesday

Important as fuck

Fucking grateful for…

"Fuck No" is a perfectly acceptable way to say "No." So is, "Fuck Nope." Sounds weird, at first, but it's oddly satisfying. Try it ;)

21 Thursday	22 Friday	23 Saturday
_____	_____	_____
_____	_____	_____
_____	_____	_____
_____	_____	_____
_____	_____	_____
_____	_____	_____
_____	_____	_____
_____	_____	○ _____
_____	_____	○ _____
_____	_____	○ _____

24 Sunday

○ _____
○ _____
○ _____
○ _____
○ _____
○ _____
○ _____
○ _____
○ _____

Notes and shit

_____

_____

_____

August 2025

25 Monday
Summer Bank Holiday (UK)

26 Tuesday

27 Wednesday

_____
_____
_____
_____
_____
_____
_____
_____
_____
_____
_____

- ◯ _____
- ◯ _____
- ◯ _____
- ◯ _____
- ◯ _____
- ◯ _____
- ◯ _____
- ◯ _____
- ◯ _____

Important as fuck

_____
_____

Fucking grateful for…

_____
_____

Your brain tries to crank up the volume on bad shit and mutes the good shit. Flip the switch on that bitch.

28 Thursday

_____
_____
_____
_____
_____
_____
_____
_____
_____
_____
_____
○ _____
○ _____
○ _____
○ _____
○ _____
○ _____
○ _____
○ _____
○ _____

29 Friday

_____
_____
_____
_____
_____
_____
_____
_____
_____
_____
_____
○ _____
○ _____
○ _____
○ _____
○ _____
○ _____
○ _____
○ _____
○ _____

30 Saturday

_____
_____
_____
_____
_____
_____
○ _____
○ _____
○ _____

31 Sunday

_____
_____
_____
_____
_____
_____
○ _____
○ _____
○ _____

Notes and shit

_____
_____
_____

September 2025

Sunday	Monday	Tuesday	Wednesday
	1 Labor Day (US, CA)	2	3
7 Father's Day (AU)	8	9	10
14	15	16	17
21	22 Fall begins (Northern Hemisphere), Rosh Hashanah begins	23	24
28	29	30 National Day for Truth and Reconciliation (CA)	

Keep going, keep growing, keep knowing your fucking worth

Thursday	Friday	Saturday	Important shit
4	5	6	_____
			_____
			_____
			_____
11	12	13	_____
			_____
			_____
			_____
Patriot Day (US)			_____
18	19	20	_____
			_____
			_____
			_____
25	26	27	_____

AUGUST 2025

S	M	T	W	T	F	S
					1	2
3	4	5	6	7	8	9
10	11	12	13	14	15	16
17	18	19	20	21	22	23
24	25	26	27	28	29	30
31						

OCTOBER 2025

S	M	T	W	T	F	S
			1	2	3	4
5	6	7	8	9	10	11
12	13	14	15	16	17	18
19	20	21	22	23	24	25
26	27	28	29	30	31	

September 2025

1 Monday
Labor Day (US, CA)

2 Tuesday

3 Wednesday

_____
_____
_____
_____
_____
_____
_____
_____
_____
_____
_____

- ○ _____
- ○ _____
- ○ _____
- ○ _____
- ○ _____
- ○ _____
- ○ _____
- ○ _____
- ○ _____

Important as fuck

_____
_____
_____

Fucking grateful for...

_____
_____
_____

You are smart, funny, and kind. And the best part is you can have a friendly chat with yourself any time you want, you lucky bitch

4 Thursday	5 Friday	6 Saturday
_____	_____	_____
_____	_____	_____
_____	_____	_____
_____	_____	_____
_____	_____	_____
_____	_____	○ _____
_____	_____	○ _____
_____	_____	○ _____

7 Sunday
Father's Day (AU)

_____

○ _____	○ _____	_____
○ _____	○ _____	_____
○ _____	○ _____	_____
○ _____	○ _____	_____
○ _____	○ _____	_____
○ _____	○ _____	○ _____
○ _____	○ _____	○ _____
○ _____	○ _____	○ _____

Notes and shit

_____
_____
_____

September 2025

8 Monday	9 Tuesday	10 Wednesday

_____
_____
_____
_____
_____
_____
_____
_____
_____
_____
_____
_____

○ _____
○ _____
○ _____
○ _____
○ _____
○ _____
○ _____
○ _____
○ _____

Important as fuck

_____
_____
_____

Fucking grateful for...

_____
_____
_____

Use your powers for good. A little villainy is fine, but mostly good. Okay bitch?

11 Thursday
Patriot Day (US)

_____
_____
_____
_____
_____
_____
_____
_____
_____
_____
_____
_____

○ _____
○ _____
○ _____
○ _____
○ _____
○ _____
○ _____
○ _____
○ _____

12 Friday

_____
_____
_____
_____
_____
_____
_____
_____
_____
_____
_____
_____

○ _____
○ _____
○ _____
○ _____
○ _____
○ _____
○ _____
○ _____
○ _____

13 Saturday

_____
_____
_____
_____
_____
_____

○ _____
○ _____
○ _____

14 Sunday

_____
_____
_____
_____
_____
_____
_____

○ _____
○ _____
○ _____

Notes and shit

_____
_____
_____

September 2025

<table>
<tr><td>15 Monday</td><td>16 Tuesday</td><td>17 Wednesday</td></tr>
</table>

15 Monday
16 Tuesday
17 Wednesday

_____
_____
_____
_____
_____
_____
_____
_____
_____
_____
_____
_____

○ _____
○ _____
○ _____
○ _____
○ _____
○ _____
○ _____
○ _____
○ _____

Important as fuck

_____
_____
_____

Fucking grateful for...

_____
_____
_____

You don't owe haters the time of day, much less your precious fucks

18 Thursday

_____
_____
_____
_____
_____
_____
_____
_____
_____
_____
_____
_____

○ _____
○ _____
○ _____
○ _____
○ _____
○ _____
○ _____
○ _____
○ _____

19 Friday

_____
_____
_____
_____
_____
_____
_____
_____
_____
_____
_____
_____

○ _____
○ _____
○ _____
○ _____
○ _____
○ _____
○ _____
○ _____
○ _____

20 Saturday

_____
_____
_____
_____
_____
_____
_____
○ _____
○ _____
○ _____

21 Sunday

_____
_____
_____
_____
_____
_____
○ _____
○ _____
○ _____

Notes and shit

_____
_____
_____

September 2025

22 Monday
Fall begins (Northern Hemisphere),
Rosh Hashanah begins

_____
_____
_____
_____
_____
_____
_____
_____
_____
_____
_____

○ _____
○ _____
○ _____
○ _____
○ _____
○ _____
○ _____
○ _____
○ _____

23 Tuesday

_____
_____
_____
_____
_____
_____
_____
_____
_____
_____
_____

○ _____
○ _____
○ _____
○ _____
○ _____
○ _____
○ _____
○ _____
○ _____

24 Wednesday

_____
_____
_____
_____
_____
_____
_____
_____
_____
_____
_____

○ _____
○ _____
○ _____
○ _____
○ _____
○ _____
○ _____
○ _____
○ _____

Important as fuck

_____
_____
_____

Fucking grateful for...

_____
_____
_____

If you were any more magical, rainbows would shoot from your ass and glitter would fly from your mouth. Not sure we need that. So you're just the perfect amount of magical.

25 Thursday

_____
_____
_____
_____
_____
_____
_____
_____
_____
_____
_____
_____
- ○ _____
- ○ _____
- ○ _____
- ○ _____
- ○ _____
- ○ _____
- ○ _____
- ○ _____
- ○ _____

26 Friday

_____
_____
_____
_____
_____
_____
_____
_____
_____
_____
_____
_____
- ○ _____
- ○ _____
- ○ _____
- ○ _____
- ○ _____
- ○ _____
- ○ _____
- ○ _____
- ○ _____

27 Saturday

_____
_____
_____
_____
_____
- ○ _____
- ○ _____
- ○ _____

28 Sunday

_____
_____
_____
_____
_____
_____
- ○ _____
- ○ _____
- ○ _____

Notes and shit

_____
_____
_____

October 2025

Sunday	Monday	Tuesday	Wednesday
SEPTEMBER 2025 S M T W T F S 1 2 3 4 5 6 7 8 9 10 11 12 13 14 15 16 17 18 19 20 21 22 23 24 25 26 27 28 29 30	**NOVEMBER 2025** S M T W T F S 1 2 3 4 5 6 7 8 9 10 11 12 13 14 15 16 17 18 19 20 21 22 23 24 25 26 27 28 29 30		**1** Yom Kippur begins
5	**6** Sukkot begins	**7**	**8**
12	**13** Columbus Day (US), Indigenous Peoples' Day (US), Thanksgiving (CA)	**14**	**15**
19	**20** Diwali begins	**21**	**22**
26	**27**	**28**	**29**

You're so fucking awesome, it's scary

Thursday	Friday	Saturday	Important shit
2	3	4	_____
			_____
			_____
			_____
9	10	11	_____
			_____
			_____
			_____
16	17	18	_____
			_____
			_____
			_____
23	24	25	_____
			_____
			_____
			_____
30	31		_____
	Halloween		_____

September-October 2025

29 Monday

_____
_____
_____
_____
_____
_____
_____
_____
_____
_____
_____

○ _____
○ _____
○ _____
○ _____
○ _____
○ _____
○ _____
○ _____
○ _____

30 Tuesday
National Day of Truth and Reconciliation (CA)

_____
_____
_____
_____
_____
_____
_____
_____
_____
_____
_____

○ _____
○ _____
○ _____
○ _____
○ _____
○ _____
○ _____
○ _____
○ _____

1 Wednesday
Yom Kippur begins

_____
_____
_____
_____
_____
_____
_____
_____
_____
_____
_____

○ _____
○ _____
○ _____
○ _____
○ _____
○ _____
○ _____
○ _____
○ _____

Important as fuck

_____
_____
_____

Fucking grateful for...

_____
_____
_____

Pretend it's fun and get it done, bitch

2 Thursday

3 Friday

4 Saturday

5 Sunday

Notes and shit

October 2025

6 Monday
Sukkot begins

_____
_____
_____
_____
_____
_____
_____
_____
_____
_____
_____
_____

○ _____
○ _____
○ _____
○ _____
○ _____
○ _____
○ _____
○ _____
○ _____

7 Tuesday

_____
_____
_____
_____
_____
_____
_____
_____
_____
_____
_____
_____

○ _____
○ _____
○ _____
○ _____
○ _____
○ _____
○ _____
○ _____
○ _____

8 Wednesday

_____
_____
_____
_____
_____
_____
_____
_____
_____
_____
_____
_____

○ _____
○ _____
○ _____
○ _____
○ _____
○ _____
○ _____
○ _____
○ _____

Important as fuck

_____
_____
_____

Fucking grateful for...

_____
_____
_____

Remember: You can love being cozy AF and still be a badass

9 Thursday

_____
_____
_____
_____
_____
_____
_____
_____
_____
_____
_____
_____
_____
_____

○ _____
○ _____
○ _____
○ _____
○ _____
○ _____
○ _____
○ _____
○ _____

10 Friday

_____
_____
_____
_____
_____
_____
_____
_____
_____
_____
_____
_____
_____
_____

○ _____
○ _____
○ _____
○ _____
○ _____
○ _____
○ _____
○ _____
○ _____

11 Saturday

_____
_____
_____
_____
_____
○ _____
○ _____
○ _____

12 Sunday

_____
_____
_____
_____
_____
○ _____
○ _____
○ _____

Notes and shit

_____
_____
_____

October 2025

13 Monday
Columbus Day (US), Indigenous Peoples' Day (US), Thanksgiving Day (CA)

14 Tuesday

15 Wednesday

Important as fuck

Fucking grateful for...

If it feels like you're having far more negative thoughts than positive ones, it's because our brains are stuck in the fucking Stone Age. (Thanks, evolution, you slow fuck.) Keep looking on the bright side. Your brain will catch up!

16 Thursday

17 Friday

18 Saturday

19 Sunday

Notes and shit

October 2025

20 Monday
Diwali begins

21 Tuesday

22 Wednesday

_____

Important as fuck

_____

Fucking grateful for…

_____

When you realize you don't have to be fucking perfect, you can be awesome

23 Thursday

_____
_____
_____
_____
_____
_____
_____
_____
_____
_____
_____
_____
○ _____
○ _____
○ _____
○ _____
○ _____
○ _____
○ _____
○ _____
○ _____

24 Friday

_____
_____
_____
_____
_____
_____
_____
_____
_____
_____
_____
○ _____
○ _____
○ _____
○ _____
○ _____
○ _____
○ _____
○ _____
○ _____

25 Saturday

_____
_____
_____
_____
_____
_____
_____
○ _____
○ _____
○ _____

26 Sunday

_____
_____
_____
_____
_____
_____
○ _____
○ _____
○ _____

Notes and shit

_____
_____
_____

October-November 2025

27 Monday	28 Tuesday	29 Wednesday
_____	_____	_____
_____	_____	_____
_____	_____	_____
_____	_____	_____
_____	_____	_____
_____	_____	_____
_____	_____	_____
_____	_____	_____
_____	_____	_____
_____	_____	_____
_____	_____	_____
_____	_____	_____
○ _____	○ _____	○ _____
○ _____	○ _____	○ _____
○ _____	○ _____	○ _____
○ _____	○ _____	○ _____
○ _____	○ _____	○ _____
○ _____	○ _____	○ _____
○ _____	○ _____	○ _____
○ _____	○ _____	○ _____
○ _____	○ _____	○ _____

Important as fuck

_____

_____

_____

Fucking grateful for...

_____

_____

_____

Treat yo' self, witch

30 Thursday

31 Friday
Halloween

1 Saturday

○
○
○

2 Sunday
Daylight Saving Time ends (US, CA)

○ ___
○ ___
○ ___
○ ___
○ ___
○ ___
○ ___
○ ___
○ ___

○ ___
○ ___
○ ___
○ ___
○ ___
○ ___
○ ___
○ ___
○ ___

○ ___
○ ___
○ ___

Notes and shit

November 2025

Sunday	Monday	Tuesday	Wednesday
OCTOBER 2025 S M T W T F S 1 2 3 4 5 6 7 8 9 10 11 12 13 14 15 16 17 18 19 20 21 22 23 24 25 26 27 28 29 30 31	**DECEMBER 2025** S M T W T F S 1 2 3 4 5 6 7 8 9 10 11 12 13 14 15 16 17 18 19 20 21 22 23 24 25 26 27 28 29 30 31		
2 Daylight Saving Time ends (US, CA)	**3**	**4** Election Day (US)	**5**
9	**10**	**11** Veterans Day (US), Remembrance Day (UK, CA, AU)	**12**
16	**17**	**18**	**19**
23	**24**	**25**	**26**
30			

Today's plan: grateful heart, clear boundaries, strong fucking language

Thursday	Friday	Saturday	Important shit
		1	_____
			_____
			_____
6	7	8	_____
			_____
			_____
13	14	15	_____
			_____
			_____
20	21	22	_____
			_____
			_____
27 Thanksgiving Day (US)	28	29	_____
			_____
			_____

November 2025

3 Monday

4 Tuesday
Election Day (US)

5 Wednesday

_____
_____
_____
_____
_____
_____
_____
_____
_____
_____
_____

○ _____
○ _____
○ _____
○ _____
○ _____
○ _____
○ _____
○ _____
○ _____

Important as fuck

_____
_____
_____

Fucking grateful for…

_____
_____
_____

Cue your favorite hype music, let it rev you up, and launch this fucking day!

6 Thursday

_____
_____
_____
_____
_____
_____
_____
_____
_____
_____
_____
_____
_____
_____

○ _____
○ _____
○ _____
○ _____
○ _____
○ _____
○ _____
○ _____
○ _____

7 Friday

_____
_____
_____
_____
_____
_____
_____
_____
_____
_____
_____
_____

○ _____
○ _____
○ _____
○ _____
○ _____
○ _____
○ _____
○ _____
○ _____

8 Saturday

_____
_____
_____
_____

○ _____
○ _____
○ _____

9 Sunday

_____
_____
_____
_____

○ _____
○ _____
○ _____

Notes and shit

_____
_____
_____

November 2025

10 Monday

_____
_____
_____
_____
_____
_____
_____
_____
_____
_____
_____

○ _____
○ _____
○ _____
○ _____
○ _____
○ _____
○ _____
○ _____
○ _____

11 Tuesday
Veterans Day (US), Remembrance
Day (UK, CA, AU)

_____
_____
_____
_____
_____
_____
_____
_____
_____
_____
_____

○ _____
○ _____
○ _____
○ _____
○ _____
○ _____
○ _____
○ _____
○ _____

12 Wednesday

_____
_____
_____
_____
_____
_____
_____
_____
_____
_____
_____

○ _____
○ _____
○ _____
○ _____
○ _____
○ _____
○ _____
○ _____
○ _____

Important as fuck

_____
_____
_____

Fucking grateful for...

_____
_____
_____

Life can be tough as Hell, and it doesn't come with instructions.
Not that you'd read them, you fucking rebel.

13 Thursday   14 Friday   15 Saturday

_____   _____   _____
_____   _____   _____
_____   _____   _____
_____   _____   _____
_____   _____   _____
_____   _____   _____
_____   _____   ○ _____
_____   _____   ○ _____
_____   _____   ○ _____
_____   _____

                                                           16 Sunday
_____   _____
_____   _____   _____
○ _____   ○ _____   _____
○ _____   ○ _____   _____
○ _____   ○ _____   _____
○ _____   ○ _____   _____
○ _____   ○ _____   _____
○ _____   ○ _____   _____
○ _____   ○ _____   ○ _____
○ _____   ○ _____   ○ _____
○ _____   ○ _____   ○ _____

Notes and shit

_____
_____
_____

November 2025

17 Monday   18 Tuesday   19 Wednesday

Important as fuck

Fucking grateful for...

Fun fact: Swearing always helps

20 Thursday   21 Friday   22 Saturday

_____   _____   _____
_____   _____   _____
_____   _____   _____
_____   _____   _____
_____   _____   _____
_____   _____   _____
_____   _____   ○ _____
_____   _____   ○ _____
_____   _____   ○ _____

23 Sunday

_____   _____
_____   _____   _____
_____   _____   _____
○ _____   ○ _____   _____
○ _____   ○ _____   _____
○ _____   ○ _____   _____
○ _____   ○ _____   _____
○ _____   ○ _____   _____
○ _____   ○ _____   ○ _____
○ _____   ○ _____   ○ _____
○ _____   ○ _____   ○ _____

Notes and shit

_____
_____
_____

November 2025

24 Monday	25 Tuesday	26 Wednesday
_____	_____	_____
_____	_____	_____
_____	_____	_____
_____	_____	_____
_____	_____	_____
_____	_____	_____
_____	_____	_____
_____	_____	_____
_____	_____	_____
_____	_____	_____
_____	_____	_____
_____	_____	_____
○ _____	○ _____	○ _____
○ _____	○ _____	○ _____
○ _____	○ _____	○ _____
○ _____	○ _____	○ _____
○ _____	○ _____	○ _____
○ _____	○ _____	○ _____
○ _____	○ _____	○ _____
○ _____	○ _____	○ _____
○ _____	○ _____	○ _____

Important as fuck

_____

_____

_____

Fucking grateful for...

_____

_____

_____

The first rule of Feast Club? Stretchy pants

27 Thursday
Thanksgiving Day (US)

_____
_____
_____
_____
_____
_____
_____
_____
_____
_____
_____
_____
- ○ _____
- ○ _____
- ○ _____
- ○ _____
- ○ _____
- ○ _____
- ○ _____
- ○ _____
- ○ _____

28 Friday

_____
_____
_____
_____
_____
_____
_____
_____
_____
_____
_____
- ○ _____
- ○ _____
- ○ _____
- ○ _____
- ○ _____
- ○ _____
- ○ _____
- ○ _____
- ○ _____

29 Saturday

_____
_____
_____
_____
_____
- ○ _____
- ○ _____
- ○ _____

30 Sunday

_____
_____
_____
_____
_____
- ○ _____
- ○ _____
- ○ _____

Notes and shit

_____
_____
_____

December 2025

Sunday	Monday	Tuesday	Wednesday
	1	2	3
7	8	9	10
14 Hanukkah begins	15	16	17
21 Winter begins (Northern Hemisphere)	22	23	24 Christmas Eve
28	29	30	31 New Year's Eve

Eat, drink and be sweary

Thursday	Friday	Saturday	Important shit
4	5	6	_____
11	12	13	_____
18	19	20	_____
25 Christmas Day	26 Boxing Day (UK, CA, AU), Kwanzaa begins	27	_____

NOVEMBER 2025

S	M	T	W	T	F	S
						1
2	3	4	5	6	7	8
9	10	11	12	13	14	15
16	17	18	19	20	21	22
23	24	25	26	27	28	29
30						

JANUARY 2026

S	M	T	W	T	F	S
				1	2	3
4	5	6	7	8	9	10
11	12	13	14	15	16	17
18	19	20	21	22	23	24
25	26	27	28	29	30	31

December 2025

1 Monday

_____
_____
_____
_____
_____
_____
_____
_____
_____
_____
_____
_____
○ _____
○ _____
○ _____
○ _____
○ _____
○ _____
○ _____
○ _____
○ _____

2 Tuesday

_____
_____
_____
_____
_____
_____
_____
_____
_____
_____
_____
_____
○ _____
○ _____
○ _____
○ _____
○ _____
○ _____
○ _____
○ _____
○ _____

3 Wednesday

_____
_____
_____
_____
_____
_____
_____
_____
_____
_____
_____
_____
○ _____
○ _____
○ _____
○ _____
○ _____
○ _____
○ _____
○ _____
○ _____

Important as fuck

_____
_____
_____

Fucking grateful for…

_____
_____
_____

You are a fucking gift! You won't fit in a stocking, though, so keep shopping, bitch.

4 Thursday

5 Friday

6 Saturday

○ _____
○ _____
○ _____

7 Sunday

○ _____
○ _____
○ _____
○ _____
○ _____
○ _____
○ _____
○ _____
○ _____

○ _____
○ _____
○ _____
○ _____
○ _____
○ _____
○ _____
○ _____
○ _____

○ _____
○ _____
○ _____

Notes and shit

_____
_____
_____

December 2025

8 Monday	9 Tuesday	10 Wednesday

Important as fuck

Fucking grateful for…

Sleigh, bitch, sleigh

11 Thursday

_____
_____
_____
_____
_____
_____
_____
_____
_____
_____
_____
_____
_____
○ _____
○ _____
○ _____
○ _____
○ _____
○ _____
○ _____
○ _____
○ _____

12 Friday

_____
_____
_____
_____
_____
_____
_____
_____
_____
_____
_____
_____
_____
○ _____
○ _____
○ _____
○ _____
○ _____
○ _____
○ _____
○ _____
○ _____

13 Saturday

_____
_____
_____
_____
_____
_____
○ _____
○ _____
○ _____

14 Sunday
Hanukkah begins

_____
_____
_____
_____
_____
○ _____
○ _____
○ _____

Notes and shit

_____
_____
_____

December 2025

15 Monday	16 Tuesday	17 Wednesday

Important as fuck

Fucking grateful for…

The Ghosts of Christmas Past, Present and Future agree: you are fucking awesome

18 Thursday

_____
_____
_____
_____
_____
_____
_____
_____
_____
_____
_____
○ _____
○ _____
○ _____
○ _____
○ _____
○ _____
○ _____
○ _____
○ _____

19 Friday

_____
_____
_____
_____
_____
_____
_____
_____
_____
○ _____
○ _____
○ _____
○ _____
○ _____
○ _____
○ _____
○ _____
○ _____

20 Saturday

_____
_____
_____
_____
_____
○ _____
○ _____
○ _____

21 Sunday
Winter begins (Northern Hemisphere)

_____
_____
_____
_____
_____
○ _____
○ _____
○ _____

Notes and shit

_____
_____
_____

December 2025

22 Monday

23 Tuesday

24 Wednesday
Christmas Eve

○
○
○
○
○
○
○
○
○

○
○
○
○
○
○
○
○
○

○
○
○
○
○
○
○
○
○

Important as fuck

Fucking grateful for...

Congratulations on making the "Nice List" <u>and</u> the "Naughty List" again this year, you merry fucking badass

25 Thursday
Christmas Day

26 Friday
Boxing Day (UK, CA, AU), Kwanzaa begins

27 Saturday

- ○
- ○
- ○

28 Sunday

(Thursday)
- ○
- ○
- ○
- ○
- ○
- ○
- ○
- ○
- ○

(Friday)
- ○
- ○
- ○
- ○
- ○
- ○
- ○
- ○
- ○

(Sunday)
- ○
- ○
- ○

Notes and shit

December 2025-January 2026

29 Monday

_____
_____
_____
_____
_____
_____
_____
_____
_____
_____
_____
_____

○ _____
○ _____
○ _____
○ _____
○ _____
○ _____
○ _____
○ _____
○ _____

30 Tuesday

_____
_____
_____
_____
_____
_____
_____
_____
_____
_____
_____
_____

○ _____
○ _____
○ _____
○ _____
○ _____
○ _____
○ _____
○ _____
○ _____

31 Wednesday
New Year's Eve

_____
_____
_____
_____
_____
_____
_____
_____
_____
_____
_____
_____

○ _____
○ _____
○ _____
○ _____
○ _____
○ _____
○ _____
○ _____
○ _____

Important as fuck

_____
_____
_____

Fucking grateful for...

_____
_____
_____

Cheers to fun that makes you laugh so hard, no sound comes out! (But a little pee might ;)

1 Thursday
New Year's Day

_____
_____
_____
_____
_____
_____
_____
_____
_____
_____
_____
_____
○ _____
○ _____
○ _____
○ _____
○ _____
○ _____
○ _____
○ _____
○ _____

2 Friday

_____
_____
_____
_____
_____
_____
_____
_____
_____
_____
_____
○ _____
○ _____
○ _____
○ _____
○ _____
○ _____
○ _____
○ _____
○ _____

3 Saturday

_____
_____
_____
_____
_____
○ _____
○ _____
○ _____

4 Sunday

_____
_____
_____
_____
_____
○ _____
○ _____
○ _____

Notes and shit

_____
_____
_____

My Brilliant Thoughts & Shit

My Brilliant Thoughts & Shit

My Brilliant Thoughts & Shit

My Brilliant Thoughts & Shit

My Brilliant Thoughts & Shit

Bonus Gifts

Hello Awesome! I hope these swear word gifts help you laugh and feel positive AF. These are high-quality PDF files that you can print at home or using a printing service. Feel free to share with friends!

What's Included

Floral Color Prints
48 Sweary affirmation cards (2.5 x 3.5 in.)

Floral Color Prints
48 Sweary wall art posters (8.5 x 11 in.)

Black and White Coloring Pages
48 Sweary quote designs (8.5 x 11 in.)

How to Access

Option 1

Scan this QR code with your device

You will see a "Download" button for instant access

—OR—

Option 2

Type this URL into your web browser:

sassyquotespress.com/2025gifts

You will see a "Download" button for instant access

—OR—

Option 3

Email me at
jen@sassyquotespress.com

I would love to hear from you! I can't promise "instant access," but I will respond ASAP!

More from Sassy Quotes Press

Check out more of our hilarious swear word planners, coloring books and gratitude journals. Available on your local Amazon marketplace.

Want freebies and updates?

Sign up for free coloring pages and more at

SASSYQUOTESPRESS.COM

Questions? Comments? I would love to hear from you! Please email me at Jen@SassyQuotesPress.com

A Favor Please!

Whether you purchased this planner or received it as a gift...

Your star rating or review of my book on Amazon makes a **HUGE** fucking difference to me as an independent publisher.

Seriously. I know your time is *valuable AF*. So, if you could take a quick minute to rate or review my book, I would *very* grateful!

Wondering how to do that?

Here are two ways:

Option 1 - If you purchased the planner

If using the Amazon Web site: Click on **Returns and Orders** on the upper right menu of the Amazon website.

If using the Amazon mobile app: Click on the person icon (👤) at the bottom of the mobile app and then click on **Your Orders** button.

You'll see **Write a Product Review** button or link next to my book. Press this button or link to leave a star rating or review.

Option 2 - If you purchased the planner <u>or received it as a gift</u>

Visit my **Sassy Quotes Press Amazon Author Page.** You can reach it by:

• Entering the following URL into your web browser:

amazon.com/author/sassyquotespress

• Or by scanning this QR code with your device:

Click on the image of the book that you own to open the product page.

Scroll down the book product page until you see the **Write a customer review** button. Press this button to leave a star rating or review.

Thank you! You are a fucking star!

Made in the USA
Columbia, SC
03 January 2025